Generational
and
Family Blessings

Generational and Family Blessings

Ruth Hawkey

New Wine Press

New Wine Ministries
PO Box 17
Chichester
West Sussex
United Kingdom
PO19 2AW

Scripture quotations are taken from New King James Version, copyright © 1983, 1992 by Thomas Nelson, Inc.

ISBN 978-1-905991-32-7

Typeset by CRB Associates, Reepham, Norfolk
Printed in Malta

Contents

Preface

A number of years ago I wrote a small book entitled *Freedom from Generational Sin*. This looked at the subject of the possible consequences of sin committed by an ancestor travelling down the family line to affect the present and future generations. The book also included how to be set free from the consequences of such sin.

Since writing that book I have also taught the opposite scriptural viewpoint that it was God's original intention for blessing to flow down a godly family line – through those who are seeking to be obedient to His will. I would like to emphasise that in this book we are looking at spiritual rather than material blessings.

Having taught this subject on a number of occasions I have been asked if the teaching is in print, hence this book. I pray that it will be a blessing and an encouragement to you that God's heart is to bless you and your children and your children's children.

Ruth Hawkey

The Father's Heart Is to Bless

The words "bless" or "blessing" occur four hundred and ten times in the Scriptures. This highlights the importance of the subject and shows us that it is in the heart of God, Creator of this world, to pour blessings upon all of His creation.

As we shall see in a later chapter the Scriptures also teach us that our Heavenly Father desires to pour blessings upon His children: those who trust in Him and have been born into His family through His Son Jesus Christ.

> *"... showing mercy to thousands, to those who love Me and keep My commandments."* (Exodus 20:6)

Truly it is God's heart to bless His world and His people. Let us briefly remind ourselves of the many ways in which God does this.

The Father's Heart Is to Bless His Creation

God spoke His world into being and then proceeded to bless that which He had created: He blessed the animals; the sea creatures; the birds; the sun, moon and stars; the rivers and waterfalls; the hills and mountains; the flowers and trees; all of His creation rests in the blessing of His continuing mercy and care. According to Lamentations 3:23 we are assured that God's compassion and mercy never fails:

> *"They are new every morning;*
> *Great is Your faithfulness."*

We are also told in Genesis 1:21–22 that:

> *"God created great sea creatures and every living thing that moves, with which the waters abounded, according to their kind, and every winged bird according to its kind. And God saw that it was good. And God blessed them ... "*

How exciting it is to remember, when we look around at our world, that it is a place which is under God's blessing.

We are also reminded in Genesis 1:27–28 that God also created and blessed mankind:

> *"So God created man in His own image; in the image of God He created him; male and female He created them. Then God blessed them ... "*

From the Scriptures we can also see that it is God's heart to multiply all of these blessings down through the generational line to all of His people:

> *"And God blessed them, saying, 'Be fruitful and multiply, and fill the waters in the seas ... ' "*   (Genesis 1:22)

The Blessing of God Is Shown by the Variety of His Creation

When we look at the world which God has created we are also reminded of the fact that God our Father loves variety and individuality. His blessing rests upon a wealth of multiplicity. We only have to look at the colour, the beauty and the diversity of nature, the appeal to the senses of the different seasons and the uniqueness of people and variety of cultures to realise what an amazing Creator our Father God is. Trees, animals, flowers, birds, people, fish and flowers all speak of a God who loves our individuality and wants to bless it. To realise that you are unique and priceless – one who is made in God's image – is a deep truth to be treasured.

The Blessing of the Father's Sustaining Grace

As well as God enjoying variety and blessing our uniqueness, it is also important to remember that it is God who blesses us by keeping the stars in place; whose command keeps the sea within its allocated boundaries; whose laws of the universe continue year after year and whose love is new every morning. God "spoke" the world into being and the world, as we know it, could just as easily be "unspoken". In fact, we rely on the very nature of God for the sustaining and continuance of His creation.

The Blessing of Being Able to Rely on the Very Nature of God

We are told in the Scriptures that **God's Name** and all which that entails continues throughout all generations:

"Your name, O LORD, endures forever,
Your fame, O LORD, throughout all generations."

(Psalm 135:13)

When Moses asked God what he should call Him, God answered:

" 'I AM WHO I AM.' And He said, 'Thus you shall say to the children of Israel, "I AM has sent me to you." ' "   (Exodus 3:14)

In other words God's name is eternal and we can rest on the fact that He never changes.

We are also encouraged to rely on the truth that because of **God's mercy** we are not consumed:

"Through the LORD's mercies we are not consumed,
Because His compassions fail not.
They are new every morning . . . "   (Lamentations 3:22–23)

Thus we are blessed by the knowledge that God's **mercy** is new every morning and, as the psalmist reiterates, His mercy is also eternal:

"For the LORD is good;
His mercy is everlasting,
And His truth endures to all generations."   (Psalm 100:5)

According to the Scriptures we can also trust in the **faithfulness of God**:

"Your faithfulness endures to all generations . . . "

(Psalm 119:90)

Without God's faithfulness, mercy and sustaining grace the world as we know it would cease to exist.

The Blessing of the Sabbath Day

As well as blessing creation God has also placed a special blessing upon the Sabbath day:

> *"Then God blessed the seventh day and sanctified it, because in it He rested from all His work which God had created and made."*
>
> (Genesis 2:3)

This reminds us of the importance of having times of rest in the midst of our busy work schedules. Our Heavenly Father knows that as His children we can only sustain a certain amount of work pressure and we do well to heed His provision of the "Sabbath rest" which is meant to be a blessing and not an unnecessary interruption of the working week.

The Laws of the Universe

We need to recognise, however, that there are **certain laws linked into the Father's blessing**. Because we live in a world of cause and effect God has written certain conditions into His universe which are linked to God's ability to bless His people. For example, there is the **law of sowing and reaping**. We are told that:

> *". . . whatever a man sows, that he will also reap."*
>
> (Galatians 6:7)

God can only bless us when we sow good and honourable things into our lives.

The **law of faith** is also linked to God's blessing as Jesus demonstrated:

> *"Then He touched their eyes, saying, 'According to your faith let it be to you.'"* (Matthew 9:29)

We need to exercise our faith in a faithful God and to live in the knowledge that it is His heart to bless us.

Related to the law of blessing is the **law of obedience**. One of the conditions of God being able to bless us is that we are obedient to His commandments. We see the promise of this in Deuteronomy 28:1–2:

> *"Now it shall come to pass, if you diligently obey the voice of the LORD your God, to observe carefully all His commandments which I command you today, that the LORD your God will set you high above all nations of the earth. And all these blessings shall come upon you and overtake you, because you obey the voice of the LORD your God."*

Household Blessing

We have an abundant God; a generous Heavenly Father, whose heart is to bless His creation and especially His children as they walk according to His laws. Whilst God is committed to blessing the individual who bases his life upon God's Word and who lives according to His commandments, we shall see from the Scriptures that He also desires to bless our families.

We can see many examples of this in the Old Testament. For example, God's promise to Abraham was a promise of blessing not only to Abraham but also to Sarah and their future family:

> *"And I will bless her and also give you a son by her; then I will bless her, and she shall be a mother of nations; kings of peoples shall be from her."* (Genesis 17:16)

And in Genesis 22:17 God talks again about His multiplication of blessings to Abraham and his family:

> *"blessing I will bless you, and multiplying I will multiply your descendants as the stars of the heaven and as the sand which is on*

the seashore; and your descendants shall possess the gate of their enemies."

Another family which God chose to bless was the family of Noah, who was blessed by being saved from destruction through the flood:

"Then the LORD *said to Noah, 'Come into the ark,* **you and all your household**, *because I have seen that you are righteous before Me in this generation.'"*   (Genesis 7:1, emphasis added)

Noah was a good man and we are told that his righteousness had wonderful consequences for his whole family. The ark was not just for Noah, it was for his household. The Bible says that Noah was righteous but it says nothing about the righteousness of his family – nevertheless they were all saved. This encourages us to believe that a new believer can bring all of his family into the ark, into that position of safety. They are all meant to be partakers of God's blessing. We are told in the book of James that:

"The effective, fervent prayer of a righteous man avails much."
(James 5:16)

This suggests that God's blessing is enabled to flow to our families when we are walking according to God's laws; when we are seeking to be righteous and when we are spending time in prayer on their behalf.

Job was a man who knew the blessing of being protected by God – a fact which grieved Satan so much that he confronted God about Job's position:

"So Satan answered the LORD *and said, 'Does Job fear God for nothing?* **Have You not made a hedge around him, around his household,** *and around all that he has on every side?'"*

(Job 1:9–10, emphasis added)

Will you note that, even by Satan's own admission, Job's family had a hedge of protection around them? The Scriptures tell us that this was because Job was a righteous man who feared God:

"Then the LORD *said to Satan, 'Have you considered My servant Job, that there is none like him on the earth, a blameless and upright man, one who fears God and shuns evil?' So Satan answered the* LORD *and said, 'Does Job fear God for nothing?'"* (Job 1:8–9)

Satan then goes on to tempt Job away from faith and obedience so that the blessing of the hedge of protection could be taken away.

Another family in the Old Testament who was blessed by God was the family of a man called Obed-Edom. He was a Philistine in whose house the Ark of the Covenant rested for three months and because of this God blessed Obed-Edom's family:

"The ark of the LORD *remained in the house of Obed-Edom the Gittite three months.* **And the** LORD **blessed Obed-Edom and all his household.**" (2 Samuel 6:11, emphasis added)

The New Testament

When we look at the New Testament we see that the same pattern is repeated. It also confirms the principle that God desires to bless not only individuals, but also their families. For

example, in John's Gospel chapter 4, we have the story of the
nobleman whose son was sick. Not only was the son healed
but the nobleman's whole family were saved:

> *"And there was a certain nobleman whose son was sick at
> Capernaum. When he heard that Jesus had come out of Judea into
> Galilee, he went to Him and implored Him to come down and heal
> his son, for he was at the point of death."*   (John 4:46–47)

The story continues in verse 50:

> *"Jesus said to him, 'Go your way; your son lives.' So the man
> believed the word that Jesus spoke to him, and he went his way. And
> as he was now going down, his servants met him and told him,
> saying, 'Your son lives!' Then he inquired of them the hour when he
> got better. And they said to him, 'Yesterday at the seventh hour the
> fever left him.' So the father knew that it was at the same hour in
> which Jesus said to him, 'Your son lives.' **And he himself believed,
> and his whole household."***   (John 4:50–53, emphasis added)

Only the son was healed but the nobleman and the whole
household trusted in the Lord. Thus although only the son
received the grace of healing, nevertheless all of the family
turned to the Lord. This also tells us something about the
place of healing in evangelism.

We see the same principle at work in the family of
Cornelius when he desired the filling of the Holy Spirit. We
are told that he was:

> *"a devout man and one who feared God with all his household, who
> gave alms generously to the people, and prayed to God always."*
>   (Acts 10:2)

Cornelius was encouraged to send for Peter the Apostle:

> *"who will tell you words by which you and all your household will be saved."* (Acts 11:14, emphasis added)

So Cornelius invited his relatives, friends and family to hear Peter and it was as Peter spoke that the Holy Spirit fell upon them and all that were in the house were saved.

We see the same attitude being repeated in the family of Lydia who was baptized along with her whole household:

> *"And when she and her household were baptized, she begged us, saying, 'If you have judged me to be faithful to the Lord, come to my house and stay.' So she persuaded us."*
> (Acts 16:15, emphasis added)

When the Philippian jailor believed we are told that his family were promised salvation as well:

> *"So they said, 'Believe on the Lord Jesus Christ, and you will be saved, you and your household.'"* (Acts 16:31, emphasis added)

Was the promise to the jailor fulfilled? Yes it was:

> *"Now when he had brought them into his house, he set food before them; and he rejoiced, having believed in God with all his household."* (Acts 16:34, emphasis added)

All of Stephanas' family were saved and baptized:

> *"Yes, I also baptized the household of Stephanas."*
> (1 Corinthians 1:16, emphasis added)

As was the family of Crispus:

> *"Then Crispus, the ruler of the synagogue, **believed on the Lord***
> ***with all his household.***"   (Acts 18:8, emphasis added)

Believing by the household in those days far exceeded what we
see today. Paul prayed that the whole family of Onesiphorus
would be shown mercy – not just Onesiphorus himself:

> *"Greet Prisca and Aquila, and the household of Onesiphorus."*
>   (2 Timothy 4:19)

> *"**The Lord grant mercy to the household of Onesiphorus,** for he*
> *often refreshed me, and was not ashamed of my chain."*
>   (2 Timothy 1:16, emphasis added)

Thus we see that according to the Old and New Testaments it
is God's heart to bless not only the individual but also their
family. It could also be argued that if they had servants, which
some of them had, then the servants were included in the
blessing of salvation. This does not of course take away from
the fact or necessity of individual repentance and conversion
but rather shows what we can confidently come to God and
ask Him for our children's salvation. The words are true: *"You
have not because you ask not."* If we know that *"*family
salvation*"* is on the heart of God then we can ask more
confidently being assured that it is in accordance with His will.

Generational Blessing

According to the Scriptures God's blessing is meant to go even further that that of blessing our own personal family. God's heart is to pour His blessings down our family line to our future generations. When God's people obey God's commandments and walk in faith and obedience to them then the blessings which God confers on them are passed down the generational line and, we are told, multiplied for a thousand generations:

> *"Oh, that they had such a heart in them that they would fear Me and always keep all My commandments, that it might be well with them and with their children forever!"*   (Deuteronomy 5:29)

> *"The righteous man walks in his integrity.*
> *His children are blessed after him."*   (Proverbs 20:7)

Scripture tells us that the blessing of faith can travel down the family line and gives us the example of Timothy's inheritance of faith from his grandmother and mother:

"I call to remembrance the genuine faith that is in you, which was also in your grandmother Lois and your mother Eunice . . . "

(2 Timothy 1:5)

We are not told whether it was Timothy's grandmother on his father or his mother's side; one assumes the mother since the father is not mentioned.

We are also encouraged to believe that mercy travels down the family line, yes even the mercy of God to those who love and honour Him:

"Therefore know that the LORD your God, He is God, the faithful God who keeps covenant and mercy for a thousand generations with those who love Him and keep His commandments."

(Deuteronomy 7:9)

And, of course, we can be assured, according to the Scriptures, of God's righteousness being available for our grandchildren:

"The mercy of the LORD is from everlasting to everlasting
On those who fear Him,
And His righteousness to children's children."

(Psalm 103:17)

We see the evidence of God's blessing upon the generational line when we consider the family of Adam. When Adam sinned he forfeited his position in the Garden of Eden where he used to walk and talk with God on a regular basis. However, we can see the tremendous mercy and blessing of God upon Adam's future generational line in that one of Adam's descendants, Enoch, like Adam, also walked with God. What a blessing for Adam and Eve:

"After he begot Methuselah, Enoch walked with God three hundred years, and had sons and daughters. So all the days of Enoch were three hundred and sixty-five years. And Enoch walked with God; and he was not, for God took him."   (Genesis 5:22–24)

According to a literal interpretation of Genesis 5, the abundance of God's blessing can also be seen in the fact that God actually allowed Adam to live to see this happening as shown in Figure 1.

Figure 1: Adam's Family Line According to Genesis 5

Adam was 130 when Seth was born (v. 3) and Adam died when he was 930 (v. 5). The following table shows Adam's age when his descendants were born:

Adam's age	Descendants
235	Seth was 105 when Enosh was born (v. 6) and died when he was 912 (v. 8).
325	Enosh was 90 when Cainan was born (v. 9) and died when he was 905 (v. 11).
395	Cainan was 70 when Mahalalel was born (v. 12) and died when he was 910 (v. 14).
460	Mahalalel was 65 when Jared was born (v. 15) and died when he was 895 (v. 17).
622	Jared was 162 when Enoch was born (v. 18) and died when he was 962 (v. 20).
687	**Enoch was 65 when Methuselah was born (v. 21) but did not die for God took him when he was 365 (v. 23).**
	Methuselah was 187 when Lamech was born (v. 25) and died when he was 969 (v. 27).
	Lamech was 182 when Noah was born (v. 28) and died when he was 777 (v. 31)

Adam, if he had lived, would have been one thousand and fifty-six years old by the time Noah the son of Lamech was born, but, as we have seen, Adam died when he was nine hundred and thirty years old. Just to complete the picture Noah was over five hundred years old when Shem, Ham and Japheth were born (v. 32) and Noah died when he was nine hundred and fifty years old (Genesis 9:29).

Thus a literal interpretation would suggest that Adam was still alive (six hundred and twenty-two years old) when Enoch was born! However, according to the *New Bible Dictionary*: "genealogies, including those of Genesis 5 ... must always be used with great restraint whenever it appears that they are open to more than one interpretation".[1] The interesting point is that even though Adam sinned he still had a descendant who "walked with God" as he had! What a blessing – truly a merciful God.

Generational Blessing in Abraham's Family

As well as the family line of Adam and Eve there are many other instances of generational blessing within the Scriptures, of which perhaps the most well known is that of Abraham. God's plan to bless Abraham always included his future descendants – the Jewish people. God declared that through Isaac Abraham's descendants were going to be as numerous as the stars and that:

> "... all the nations of the earth shall be blessed, because you have obeyed My voice."   (Genesis 22:18)

The promised blessing was stated again to Abraham's son Isaac:

"I will make your descendants multiply as the stars of heaven; I will give to your descendants all these lands; and in your seed all the nations of the earth shall be blessed." (Genesis 26:4)

There came a day when God reiterates the promised blessing to Abraham's grandson Jacob. God promises him that:

"... the land on which you lie I will give to you and your descendants. Also your descendants shall be as the dust of the earth; you shall spread abroad to the west and the east, to the north and the south; and in you and in your seed all the families of the earth shall be blessed." (Genesis 28:13–14)

We don't have to look far in the Scriptures to see that the promised blessing is also there with Abraham's great grandson Joseph:

"The LORD was with Joseph, and he was a successful man; and he was in the house of his master the Egyptian ... and the blessing of the LORD was on all that he had in the house and in the field."
(Genesis 39:2, 5)

The blessing is also pronounced on Abraham's other great grandson, Judah:

"The sceptre shall not depart from Judah,
Nor a lawgiver from between his feet,
Until Shiloh comes." (Genesis 49:10)

This blessing continues down the family line to King David – who was of the family of Judah and will indeed continue into eternity.

"And your house and your kingdom shall be established forever before you. Your throne shall be established forever."   (2 Samuel 7:16)

In 2 Samuel 2:4 we read:

"Then the men of Judah came, and there they anointed David king over the house of Judah."

The blessing carries on down the generational line to Solomon and his descendants, for King David is promised that his son Solomon will know the blessing of God and that God will be his Father:

"... and I will establish the throne of his kingdom over Israel forever."   (1 Chronicles 22:10)

And of course God's promised blessings also included Jesus who was of the line of Judah:

"From this man's seed [David], according to the promise, God raised up for Israel a Saviour – Jesus."   (Acts 13:23)

God's Blessing to Descendants of Obed-Edom

We have already considered the blessing upon the household of Obed-Edom. However, the blessing didn't just rest upon him but was also evident on his sons and grandsons. They were described as men of great ability; *"able men with strength for work"*. Their history is recorded in 1 Chronicles 26:4–8:

"Moreover the sons of Obed-Edom were Shemaiah the firstborn, Jehozabad the second, Joah the third, Sacar the fourth, Nethanel the

fifth, Ammiel the sixth, Issachar the seventh, Peulthai the eighth; for God blessed him. Also to Shemaiah his son were sons born who governed their fathers' houses, because they were men of great ability. The sons of Shemaiah were Othni, Rephael, Obed, and Elzabad, whose brothers Elihu and Semachiah were able men. All these were of the sons of Obed-Edom, they and their sons and their brethren, able men with strength for the work: sixty-two of Obed-Edom."

More Old Testament Examples of Generational Blessing

Phinehas was another man whose generational line knew a great deal about the blessing of God. He was the son of Eleazar and the grandson of Aaron:

"Eleazar, Aaron's son, took for himself one of the daughters of Putiel as wife; and she bore him Phinehas." (Exodus 6:25)

In Numbers 25:7–13 we have the story of Phinehas who saved the Israelites from the plague. An Israelite had sinned by marrying a foreign wife. Phinehas killed both the woman and the Israelite and thus turned away God's judgment from the nation. The Psalms also record this vital part of Israel's history:

"Then Phinehas stood up and intervened,
And the plague was stopped.
And that was accounted to him for righteousness
To all generations forevermore." (Psalm 106:30–31)

Ezra, who was a descendant of Aaron and Phinehas, also walked in his ancestors' blessing:

> *"Now after these things, in the reign of Artaxerxes king of Persia,*
> *Ezra the son of . . . Phinehas, the son of Eleazar, the son of Aaron the*
> *chief priest . . . the hand of the* LORD *his God upon him."*
>
> (Ezra 7:1, 5–6)

When we turn to the book of Ezra we can read the tremendous account of Ezra's contribution to Israel's history and there we see how God's blessing continued down his family line.

Caleb was a man who God promised to bless because he was a man after God's own heart: a man of a different spirit. He was one of the two spies who brought back a good report, with Joshua, concerning the land of Canaan. He declared to Moses that he truly believed that God would give them the land. As we can see from the Scriptures, God, because of Caleb's faith, promised to bless his descendants as well.

> *"But My servant Caleb, because he has a different spirit in him and*
> *has followed Me fully, I will bring into the land where he went, and*
> *his descendants shall inherit it."*   (Numbers 14:24)

Caleb's nephew was one of the descendants upon whom God bestowed His blessing: he turned out to be a very good judge in Israel:

> *"When the children of Israel cried out to the* LORD, *the* LORD *raised*
> *up a deliverer for the children of Israel, who delivered them: Othniel*
> *the son of Kenaz, Caleb's younger brother. The Spirit of the* LORD
> *came upon him, and he judged Israel."*   (Judges 3:9–10)

It is interesting to note that in Caleb's line there was also a man called Nabal; he was the person who refused to help King

David when he was in real need (1 Samuel 25). Nabal was very rich and prosperous but nevertheless he was also very stubborn and it was his wife Abigail who eventually helped David and became David's wife after Nabal died. (What was strength in Caleb – his determination – became a weakness in Nabal resulting in his stubbornness.)

Another generational line which was blessed by God was the family line of Rahab. In Joshua chapter 6 we read how Rahab took care of the two spies Joshua had sent into Jericho to look over the land, prior to Joshua's armies moving in to do battle. She hid the spies on the roof of her house and was told to hang a scarlet thread out of the window of her house in order to remain safe. Everyone would be killed in Jericho except those within her house.

> *"So it shall be that whoever goes outside the doors of your house into the street, his blood shall be on his own head, and we will be guiltless. And whoever is with you in the house, his blood shall be on our head if a hand is laid on him."* (Joshua 2:19)

Rahab obeyed Joshua's instructions and she and all her household were saved when the walls of Jericho fell down. Rahab's future generational line is a very interesting one indeed, for she eventually married a man named Salmon:

> *"Salmon begot Boaz by Rahab, Boaz begot Obed by Ruth, Obed begot Jesse, and Jesse begot David the king. David the king begot Solomon by her who had been the wife of Uriah."* (Matthew 1:5–6)

Eventually, of course, the family line included Joseph the husband of Mary. This encourages us to believe that God can redeem and bless any family line that is willing to turn to Him and walk in His way.

According to the Scriptures other people can also be blessed because of God's righteous people: Jacob's uncle Laban asked Jacob to stay around because, as he says:

> *"I have learned by experience that the LORD has blessed me for your*
> *sake."*   (Genesis 30:27)

Potiphar was another person who became aware that his family was being blessed because of someone else, in this case Joseph:

> *"So it was, from the time that he had made him overseer of his house*
> *... that the LORD blessed the Egyptian's house for Joseph's sake."*
>   (Genesis 39:5)

This would seem to suggest that God's blessing has the potential of extending around a person to those within his work place or his extended family; in fact to any who come into contact with him in his wider sphere of influence.

Notes_____

1. *New Bible Dictionary*, Inter-Varsity Press, 1975, p. 213.

Extent of God's Blessing

The question then arises as to what exactly do the Scriptures teach us concerning the extent of God's blessing upon the family and the future generational line? We will just consider one or two of the most obvious.

Salvation for the Family

According to Moses the Passover was something which was to be remembered and celebrated for the whole family. He writes that the Paschal lamb was for the household, not just for the individual:

> "Speak to all the congregation of Israel, saying: 'On the tenth day of this month every man shall take for himself a lamb, according to the house of his father, a lamb for a household.' "
>
> (Exodus 12:3)

Thus we see that the lamb was slain for the whole house and its blood put on the doorposts. Salvation was for the household:

> *"And they shall take some of the blood and put it on the two
> doorposts and on the lintel of the houses where they eat it."*
>
> (Exodus 12:7)

It reminds one of the household of Rahab where everyone
who stayed in the house was saved. Thus we could argue that
it is God's heart and intention to save families as well as
individuals.

Peace to the Family

When Jesus sent His disciples out to the surrounding towns
and villages to preach the Gospel, He gave them some
very specific directions, which included speaking peace upon
the family with whom they stayed – not just upon the
individual:

> *"Now whatever city or town you enter, inquire who in it is worthy,
> and stay there till you go out. And when you go into a household,
> greet it. If the household is worthy, let your peace come upon it. But
> if it is not worthy, let your peace return to you."*
>
> (Matthew 10:11–13)

The Outpouring of the Holy Spirit upon the Generational Line

We are very aware that according to the sermon of Peter the
Apostle, on the Day of Pentecost, the outpouring of the Holy
Spirit was to be for the family as well as for the individual:

> *"For the promise is to you and to your children, and to all who are
> afar off, as many as the Lord our God will call."*   (Acts 2:39)

It is especially important that heads of families take a hold of this promise and align their heart with God's heart, praying for their children to enter into the promise and experience of the Holy Spirit as well as themselves. Remember that His promise is to your children as well as to yourself.

We have been considering the fact that it is possible for spiritual blessings to travel down the family line but there are of course other blessings which it is possible to see repeated within the generational line; some of these could be described as Christian virtues whilst others are moral virtues. For example, in my family line there are at least five generations of Christians, which could be due to the faithfulness, the prayers and the righteousness of someone way back in my generational line. In other words no room for boasting or of a feeling of superiority!

I recently met a young woman in the Highlands of Scotland whose grandfather had waited on the quayside to pick up Duncan Campbell from the ferry when he visited the Isle of Lewis. It was through Duncan Campbell's ministry that a tremendous revival broke out. I soon discovered that this young girl had a great gift of prayer, a remarkable gift of intercession and a throbbing heartbeat for her native Scotland. Truly a blessing which had passed down from grandfather to granddaughter.

A gentleman who works in a Christian Ministry Centre shared with me recently that there have been members of his family, over many generations, who have been involved in missionary work in South Africa as well as in Rwanda – from his great, great, great grandparents up to the present day.

One of the Christian virtues present in abundance in our family line is that of joy and laughter. If my two sisters, my mother, my daughters and my grandchildren meet together I can guarantee that within two minutes there will be gales of laughter echoing throughout the house. In fact, we were at a niece's wedding just recently and one of the distant neighbours remarked that she could hear shouts of laughter from the top of the street!

On the other hand, someone might see that there are moral virtues such as courage, strength in adversity, kindness, dependability and loyalty repeatedly present in their family line. Others might see the blessings of creativity, music, the love of the outdoors, evident amongst their family members both present and past.

The Christian family is blessed, of course, because of the obedience of Jesus. According to Deuteronomy God says:

> *"I set before you today a blessing and a curse: the blessing, if you obey the commandments of the LORD your God which I command you today."*   (Deuteronomy 11:26–27)

And the good news is that Jesus as Head of our family has:

> *"... humbled Himself and became obedient to the point of death."*
> (Philippians 2:8)

And therefore, because of His obedience, we have been blessed:

> *"... with every spiritual blessing in the heavenly places in Christ."*
> (Ephesians 1:3)

According to D.M. Lloyd-Jones in his book *God's Ultimate Purpose*[1] Paul is encouraging the Christians in Ephesus (and of course ourselves) to enter into the heritage won for us by

Jesus and thus enjoy the Christian life as we should. He argues that before the world was created God drew up a great Covenant of Grace – God the Father said that He would grant forgiveness, reconciliation, restoration, new life and a new nature to all who belonged to His Son. The condition was that the Son would come into the world and bear the sin of mankind. Through His perfect obedience to the Father He was able to do this and thus, because of His obedience, we have the right to enter into the spiritual blessings which Jesus has won for us.

What are the spiritual blessings to which Paul is referring?

According to Francis Frangipane in his book *The Power of Covenant Prayer*[2] it is "everything we behold in the life of Jesus: the blessing of healing, and miracles, of virtue and deliverance."

The following are some of the many spiritual blessings which are part of the inheritance of those who belong to the Body of Christ. For example, we have the privilege of having been **chosen**:

> *"Blessed be the God and Father of our Lord Jesus Christ, who has blessed us with every spiritual blessing in the heavenly places in Christ, just as He chose us in Him before the foundation of the world."*
>
> (Ephesians 1:3–4)

We can know the blessing of **salvation** because of Jesus:

> *"For God so loved the world that He gave His only begotten Son, that whoever believes in Him should not perish but have everlasting life."* (John 3:16)

Another wonderful blessing is that of knowing the joy of **forgiveness**:

"If we confess our sins, He is faithful and just to forgive us our sins and to cleanse us from all unrighteousness."   (1 John 1:9)

We also are blessed to know that 'in Christ' we are **new creations**:

"Therefore, if anyone is in Christ, he is a new creation; old things have passed away; behold, all things have become new."

(2 Corinthians 5:17)

Remember also that because of Jesus we have been **adopted** into God's family – what a blessing:

"For you did not receive the spirit of bondage again to fear, but you received the Spirit of adoption by whom we cry out, 'Abba, Father.' The Spirit Himself bears witness with our spirit that we are children of God, and if children, then heirs – heirs of God and joint heirs with Christ."   (Romans 8:15–17)

We have also been wonderfully **justified** because of what Jesus accomplished for us upon the cross:

"Therefore let it be known to you, brethren, that through this Man is preached to you the forgiveness of sins; and by Him everyone who believes is justified from all things from which you could not be justified by the law of Moses."   (Acts 13:38–39)

We can also know the amazing **peace** of Jesus within our hearts no matter what situations we are called upon to walk through:

"Therefore, having been justified by faith, we have peace with God through our Lord Jesus Christ, through whom also we have access by faith into this grace in which we stand."   (Romans 5:1–2)

And of course we can continually know the blessing of being **filled with the Holy Spirit** and all that is included in that blessing:

> *"But you shall receive power when the Holy Spirit has come upon you."* (Acts 1:8)

Therefore, we can know **His power, presence, gifts and fruit** – what a joy and what blessings are ours because of the obedience of Jesus. And joy of joys, blessing upon blessing, wonder upon wonders, because of Jesus we are also **glorified** in Him:

> *"Moreover whom He predestined, these He also called; whom He called, these He also justified; and whom He justified, these He also glorified."* (Romans 8:30)

Thus we have seen that it is God's heart is to bless His creation, individuals, families and future generations. However, as we have already noted there are certain conditions to be fulfilled in order for this to happen – faith and obedience seem to be key factors. It also appears to be necessary for a choice to be made by a person in authority within the household to follow God's commandments such as Joshua did when he challenged the Israelites:

> *"... choose for yourselves this day whom you will serve, whether the gods which your fathers served that were on the other side of the River, or the gods of the Amorites, in whose land you dwell. But as for me and my house, we will serve the LORD."* (Joshua 24:15)

Or as God testified about Abraham:

> *"For I have known him, in order that he may command his children and his household after him, that they keep the way of the LORD, to do righteousness and justice, that the LORD may bring to Abraham what He has spoken to him."*   (Genesis 18:19)

Or as Jacob commanded his family:

> *"And Jacob said to his household and to all who were with him, 'Put away the foreign gods that are among you, purify yourselves, and change your garments.' "*   (Genesis 35:2)

The "person in authority" would seem to be a husband, a wife or a single person who truly chooses to follow the Lord. According to Paul, writing to the Corinthians, he states that:

> *"The unbelieving husband is sanctified by the wife, and the unbelieving wife is sanctified by the husband; otherwise your children would be unclean, but now they are holy."*
> (1 Corinthians 7:14)

When we consider the story of Lydia, who was a single business woman, it would appear that a single person has the same position of authority within the household:

> *"Now a certain woman named Lydia heard us. She was a seller of purple from the city of Thyatira, who worshipped God. The Lord opened her heart to heed the things spoken by Paul. And when she and her household were baptized, she begged us, saying, 'If you have judged me to be faithful to the Lord, come to my house and stay.' "*
> (Acts 16:14–15)

Or even the story of Rahab whose family were saved because of her faith:

> *"So the men said to her: 'We will be blameless of this oath of yours which you have made us swear, unless, when we come into the land, you bind this line of scarlet cord in the window through which you let us down, and unless you bring your father, your mother, your brothers, and all your father's household to your own home. So it shall be that whoever goes outside the doors of your house into the street, his blood shall be on his own head, and we will be guiltless. And whoever is with you in the house, his blood shall be on our head if a hand is laid on him.'"* (Joshua 2:17–19)

With such examples we can be sure that God is looking for someone in the family line who is committed, faithful and obedient to Him, whatever their status in the world's eyes.

The following is the story of two families as quoted in Tim and Bev LaHaye's book *Spirit Controlled Family*.[3] The first family was descended from Max Jukes from New York State who did not believe in Christian training. He was married to a girl of like mind. One thousand and twenty-six descendants were studied. It was found that three hundred descendants had died prematurely. One hundred were in jail for an average of thirteen years each. One hundred and ninety of their descendants became prostitutes. One hundred became drunkards. All together they cost the state of New York six million dollars. This was in 1978. They made no positive contribution to society.

The second family is that of a man called Jonathan Edwards who was from same state of New York. He also married a girl of like mind but this time they both believed in Christian training. Of seven hundred and twenty-nine descendants studied they found that there were three hundred preachers of the Gospel. There were sixty-five college professors and thirteen university presidents. Sixty of Jonathan's descendants were authors of good books. Three actually became USA Congressmen and one became a Vice-President of the United States of America. There is no record of Jonathan Edwards' family having cost the state anything. Rather, they made a strong positive contribution to society.

Does God want to bless you and your family? The answer from the Scriptures would definitely appear to be yes, if we put our faith in the Lord Jesus Christ and seek to obey God's commandments. Sometimes a "family tree" helps us to see what blessings God has, and is, causing to flow down our family line – you might like to copy and use the diagram in Figure 2 opposite.

Notes _____

1. D.M. Lloyd-Jones, *God's Ultimate Purpose*, Banner of Truth Trust, 1978.
2. Francis Frangipane, *The Power of Covenant Prayer*, Charisma House, America, 1998.
3. Tim and Bev Lahaye, *Spirit Controlled Family*, Kingsway Publications, 1978.

GREAT GRANDPARENTS

Paternal

Grandfather & Grandmother
Grandfather & Grandmother

Maternal

Grandfather & Grandmother
Grandfather & Grandmother

GRANDPARENTS

Grandfather   Grandmother

Grandfather   Grandmother

PARENTS

Father

Mother

SELF

SIBLING

Figure 2: Generational Blessing

Hindrances to God's Blessing

We have already noted some of the requirements that need to be fulfilled in order for God's blessing to pass down the generational line. The importance of sowing good qualities into the family line, the importance of having faith in our Heavenly Father who works all things together for our good, as well as the importance of having a heart of obedience towards His commandments, are a great foundation. We can see also the reverse, that disobedience and unbelief are key hindrances to receiving blessing, because God has stressed that the opposite is so necessary. We are told in the Scriptures that:

> *"without faith it is impossible to please Him, for he who comes to God must believe that He is, and that He is a rewarder of those who diligently seek Him."*   (Hebrews 11:6)

Unbelief seems to hinder God's work in every area of our lives, for He is looking for those who will trust Him even through dark and difficult times. Such people choose to believe that

God is at work behind the scenes even though they cannot see the outcome, and that He will indeed work all things together for good.

An instance of this would be the family of King Hezekiah: it would seem that this man's godly heritage was at risk of faltering because of his son Manasseh:

> *"Manasseh was twelve years old when he became king, and he reigned fifty-five years in Jerusalem. But he did evil in the sight of the* LORD, *according to the abominations of the nations whom the* LORD *had cast out before the children of Israel. For he rebuilt the high places which Hezekiah his father had broken down; he raised up altars for the Baals, and made wooden images; and he worshipped all the host of heaven and served them. He also built altars in the house of the* LORD, *of which the* LORD *had said, 'In Jerusalem shall My name be forever.' And he built altars for all the host of heaven in the two courts of the house of the* LORD. *Also he caused his sons to pass through the fire in the Valley of the Son of Hinnom; he practised soothsaying, used witchcraft and sorcery, and consulted mediums and spiritists. He did much evil in the sight of the* LORD, *to provoke Him to anger. He even set a carved image, the idol which he had made, in the house of God, of which God had said to David and to Solomon his son, 'In this house and in Jerusalem, which I have chosen out of all the tribes of Israel, I will put My name forever; and I will not again remove the foot of Israel from the land which I have appointed for your fathers – only if they are careful to do all that I have commanded them, according to the whole law and the statutes and the ordinances by the hand of Moses.' So Manasseh seduced Judah and the inhabitants of Jerusalem to do more evil than the nations whom the* LORD *had destroyed before the children of Israel. And the* LORD *spoke to Manasseh and his people, but they would not listen."*   (2 Chronicles 33:1–10)

What a dreadful scenario – surely God will wipe out Hezekiah's family line; the blessing must stop with Hezekiah. However, we go on to read that Manasseh repented and God did, in His mercy, restore him:

> *"Now when he was in affliction, he implored the* LORD *his God, and humbled himself greatly before the God of his fathers, and prayed to Him; and He received his entreaty, heard his supplication, and brought him back to Jerusalem into his kingdom. Then Manasseh knew that the* LORD *was God."*
>
> (2 Chronicles 33:12–13)

So whilst we may become disillusioned concerning our family line and begin to move in unbelief when we fail to see God's hand of blessing upon our present generation, we need to remember that our future descendants may be the ones to reap the consequences of our faithfulness and obedience.

We should not allow unbelief to hinder us, or our future descendants, from receiving what God desires to give to us. If one generation turns away from God's ways that in itself is not sufficient to make a judgment against generational blessing as a whole. However, we need to be aware that when an attitude of unbelief takes root it has the potential of hindering the flow of God's blessing and somewhere in the generational line there will need to be repentance and forgiveness.

There are a number of other hindrances to receiving the blessing of God: for example, that of disdaining God's blessing; dishonouring of God; ignoring our pledge to others; not caring for widows and orphans and robbing God of His dues.

Disdaining God's Blessing

An example of the latter is one of the most difficult stories in the Scriptures as regards an obstacle to God blessing His people: the story of Esau and Jacob. According to Malachi 1:2–3 we read that God says that He loved Jacob and hated Esau:

> *"Yet Jacob I have loved;*
> *But Esau I have hated."*   (Malachi 1:2–3)

It is difficult to relate this scripture to the view that God's desire is to bless all of His children. According to R.T. Kendall the use of *love* and *hate* is a common Hebraic idiom which is not meant to be taken literally but is given as a comparison. Thus the meaning would be simply that Jacob "was preferred" over Esau. However, this doesn't alter the fact that God chooses some people to pour His blessing upon more than others. There is something here about the sovereignty of God.

When we compare this scripture with Hebrews 12:15–17 we can maybe glimpse some understanding of God's reasoning:

> *"looking carefully lest anyone fall short of the grace of God; lest any root of bitterness springing up cause trouble, and by this many become defiled; lest there be any fornicator or profane person like Esau, who for one morsel of food sold his birthright. For you know that afterward, when he wanted to inherit the blessing, he was rejected, for he found no place for repentance, though he sought it diligently with tears."*

Esau had voluntarily chosen to give up his birthright and live for present gratification, thus forfeiting God's special favour. It is quite interesting to note that Martin Luther said that he expected to see Esau in heaven, i.e. that the fact that God preferred Jacob did not mean that Esau was not loved but rather that God had a special love for Israel.

Dishonouring God

Dishonouring God is another way of hindering God's blessings. This is described in Malachi 2:1–2:

> " 'And now, O priests, this commandment is for you.
> If you will not hear,
> And if you will not take it to heart,
> To give glory to My name,'
> Says the LORD of hosts,
> 'I will send a curse upon you,
> And I will curse your blessings.
> Yes, I have cursed them already,
> Because you do not take it to heart.
> Behold, I will rebuke your descendants.' "

God is only able to bless those people who honour His name. Most of us will have seen the film *Chariots of Fire* which tells the story of one man who chose to forego fame, if necessary, in order to honour the Lord and the Sabbath day.

Conversely, we have the story of Eli the Priest who honoured his sons before God and suffered the consequences:

> "Therefore the LORD God of Israel says: 'I said indeed that your house and the house of your father would walk before Me forever.' But now the LORD says: 'Far be it from Me; for those who honour Me I will honour, and those who despise Me shall be lightly esteemed.' "
>
> (1 Samuel 2:30)

The Scriptures affirm that if we do not honour God then a curse will replace the blessing:

> *" 'And now, O priests, this commandment is for you.*
> *If you will not hear,*
> *And if you will not take it to heart,*
> *To give glory to My name,'*
> *Says the* LORD *of hosts,*
> *'I will send a curse upon you,*
> *And I will curse your blessings.*
> *Yes, I have cursed them already,*
> *Because you do not take it to heart.' "*   (Malachi 2:1–2)

It is interesting that these words are addressed to a person who has been placed in a position of authority, a priest, and therefore whose words, as we will see in a moment, have the potential of having a deep influence over the congregation.

Ignoring Our Pledge to Others

An example of this would be the covenant which Joshua made with the Gibeonites that the Israelites would always protect them:

> *"So Joshua made peace with them, and made a covenant with them*
> *to let them live; and the rulers of the congregation swore to them."*
> (Joshua 9:15)

The fact that they were trapped into this covenant by the Gibeonites made no difference to the Lord when Saul in later years broke the covenant. God brought a famine upon the land – a curse instead of a blessing:

"Now there was a famine in the days of David for three years, year after year; and David inquired of the LORD. And the LORD answered, 'It is because of Saul and his bloodthirsty house, because he killed the Gibeonites.' " (2 Samuel 21:1)

This shows how seriously God takes a covenant which is made either between God and His people or between each other.

Not Caring for Widows and Orphans

Another blockage to staying in God's blessing would seem to be if we neglect to care for the poor, the widows and the orphans. As the prophet Isaiah writes:

" 'Learn to do good;
Seek justice,
Rebuke the oppressor;
Defend the fatherless,
Plead for the widow.
Come now, and let us reason together,'
Says the LORD,
'Though your sins are like scarlet,
They shall be as white as snow;
Though they are red like crimson,
They shall be as wool.
If you are willing and obedient,
You shall eat the good of the land;
But if you refuse and rebel,
You shall be devoured by the sword';
For the mouth of the LORD has spoken." (Isaiah 1:17–20)

Robbing God of His Dues

Finally the Scriptures teach us that paying tithes is a requisite of living under God's blessing.

> " 'Will a man rob God?
> Yet you have robbed Me!
> But you say,
> "In what way have we robbed You?"
> In tithes and offerings.
> You are cursed with a curse,
> For you have robbed Me,
> Even this whole nation.
> Bring all the tithes into the storehouse,
> That there may be food in My house,
> And try Me now in this,'
> Says the LORD of hosts,
> 'If I will not open for you the windows of heaven
> And pour out for you such blessing
> That there will not be room enough to receive it.
> And I will rebuke the devourer for your sakes,
> So that he will not destroy the fruit of your ground,
> Nor shall the vine fail to bear fruit for you in the field,'
> Says the LORD of hosts."   (Malachi 3:8–11)

Some people argue that tithing is an Old Testament principle and that Christians are under a new covenant and therefore do not need to give a tenth of their income to the Lord. There appear to be reasonable arguments on both sides of the debate, although as Christians it would seem to be apposite that all that we are and have belongs to the Lord and therefore at least a tenth would be given to church or charities. We have already seen that one of the laws of blessing is the law of sowing and reaping. I believe that this law is linked into the question of tithing.

According to the New Testament, if we sow sparingly then we will certainly reap sparingly, and conversely if we sow generously then we will certainly reap generously.

> *"But this I say: He who sows sparingly will also reap sparingly, and he who sows bountifully will also reap bountifully. So let each one give as he purposes in his heart, not grudgingly or of necessity; for God loves a cheerful giver. And God is able to make all grace abound toward you, that you, always having all sufficiency in all things, may have abundance for every good work."*
>
> (2 Corinthians 9:6–8)

We are also reminded in the Scriptures that we cannot out-give God:

> *"Give, and it will be given to you: good measure, pressed down, shaken together, and running over will be put into your bosom. For with the same measure that you use, it will be measured back to you."*
>
> (Luke 6:38)

Made in the Image of God

We have seen that it is the intention of God's heart to bless His creation, His people and their present-day families as well as their future generational lines. I firmly believe that it is also the intention of God's heart that we, His children, bless other people. This may be by our presence (being salt and light in the world) as well as by our actions towards other people. Another way in which we do this is through our words.

According to the book of Proverbs there is a great deal of power in the words which we speak. These can be either for good or ill. The writer of Proverbs states:

> *"Death and life are in the power of the tongue."*
>
> (Proverbs 18:21)

From this scripture we can see that we can either bless others by speaking life into them or conversely curse them by speaking death into their spirits. Why is this so? I believe that there are two main reasons – the place of authority and the source from which they proceed.

Authority to Bless

The first and most important one is that of the position of authority which lies behind the one speaking the words. The Scriptures affirm that it is out of the heart that the mouth speaks and if the person who is speaking is in a position of authority over us, then their words will carry great power. For example, parents hold a tremendous place of authority in a child's life and therefore the words which they speak have the potential of making a deep and lasting impression upon the child, either for good or ill. The power of the word lies in the authority which lies behind the word. This is true either of blessing or of curse: authority is the key.

God-given Delegated Authority

In the Scriptures men and women of faith knew the importance of being placed in a position of authority in order that they might speak out the truth which God had commanded them to declare. Take, for example, the faith which Abraham showed when he spoke words concerning his son Isaac:

> *"And Abraham said to his young men, 'Stay here with the donkey; the lad and I will go yonder and worship, **and we will come back to you**.'"*   (Genesis 22:5, emphasis added)

Moses showed a similar faith when faced with the dilemma of the Red Sea:

> *"And Moses said to the people, 'Do not be afraid. **Stand still, and see the salvation of the** LORD, which He will accomplish for you today."*   (Exodus 14:13, emphasis added)

Likewise when Joshua was faced with having to attack Jericho before the walls fell down he was given authority by the Lord to address the walls of Jericho:

> *"And the LORD said to Joshua: 'See! I have given Jericho into your hand.'"* (Joshua 6:2)

Also when David confronted Goliath he knew that his authority was centred upon the Lord:

> *"This day the LORD will deliver you into my hand, and I will strike you and take your head from you."* (1 Samuel 17:46)

And certainly Elijah was aware of his delegated authority when yet again he confronted Ahab:

> *"As the LORD God of Israel lives, before whom I stand, there shall not be dew nor rain these years, except at my word."* (1 Kings 17:1)

Thus men of faith knew the necessity of speaking out what God had already spoken to them.

Delegated Authority by Society

As well as God delegating authority to certain people, so also does the society in which we live. For example, when a policeman stops you on the motorway for a motoring offence and commands you to pull over immediately, you promptly obey his words because he is in a position of authority, an authority delegated by society.

Teachers are also given authority by the community and as such are in an excellent position to speak words of blessing or cursing upon the children who are in their care. Truly they are *in locus parentis* (they have the delegated authority instead of a parent when they are teaching) and as such their words can be very powerful in the life of a child in much the same way as a parent's would be.

An article in the *Sunday Times*, on 25th July 2004, includes an extract from *The Boy with no Shoes* by the author William Horwood. This article gives a very apt description of the power of words to bless and encourage others. The well known children's writer tells how it was the words of a very special teacher who helped to drag him out of a sense of failure because of bullying and family rejection. William was terrified of examinations and especially became very frightened at the thought of taking the 11 plus examination after some very poor teaching.

On the night before the test his granny put some confidence into him through her words of encouragement. However, it was only after a new English master was put in charge of his class that he truly began to make remarkable progress. William writes about the way in which the new English master introduced himself:

> " 'This is the first lesson I have ever taught anyone,' he said, 'which means all of us, you and I, have ... that we all have everything to gain.' It was the first positive thing any master had said to us.
>
> 'Now,' he said, 'I have been told that as a class you are "not very good at English" and might find O-levels "difficult". Let us deal with this misconception at once.' We stared. 'Do you realize that adults come from all over the world to England to learn English? And they find English very difficult. But I doubt that a single one of those adults would be able to speak

English even half as well as each one of you already do. In short ... each one of you is an expert at English language, so good in fact that people would pay each of you a great deal of money if you could teach them what you know.'

We sat thunderstruck.

'So I see no reason why in eight months' time you shouldn't pass your English language O-level.'

'But, sir?' It was Jowett. 'O-levels aren't, er, simple, are they?'

'Oh, but they are, Jowett, they are very simple. People like to make examinations seem difficult but really they are not. Now, repeat after me: "I am going to pass my O-level in English language next year."' We mumbled the words.

'Louder, please,' he said.

Soon we were roaring: 'I AM GOING TO PASS MY O-LEVEL ENGLISH LANGUAGE NEXT YEAR!'

The classroom door slammed open and Captain Flax stood there. 'What ... ' he began, ' ... is going on?' Mr Wharton's eyes grew steely behind his spectacles.

'I am very sorry if we have disturbed you, Captain Flax. Youthful enthusiasm ... '

Then he did the unthinkable: he turned back to us and somehow consigned Captain Flax to the shadows. The door closed. Mr Wharton glanced towards it with the briefest of looks of intense dislike.

'Before this lesson ends,' he told us, 'I want to make something clear. There is an expectation that the pass rate in this class will not be high. But I do not like failure, because generally it is completely unnecessary.

'More importantly, I like the feeling of success. It breeds more success. I have very little interest in how this class may perform in other subjects, but in my subjects this form will do better than the Upper Fifth, better ... '

Looking at our astonished faces, he said: 'But I see you do not believe that as a form you will do as well as the Upper Fifth. But you will succeed. One by one you will succeed just as, a long time ago, I began to succeed after a long time of not doing so.' "

What a wonderful description of the power of someone in a position of authority, using their ability to speak words of encouragement and blessing in order that a child could move from a position of failure to a place of success.

God's Inherent Authority

God, of course, has absolute inherent authority and we can see evidence of this through His spoken word at creation. We are told in the Scriptures that in the beginning God created the world through His Word – the uncreated Creator created out of His spirit through His Word:

> *"By faith we understand that the worlds were framed by the word of God, so that the things which are seen were not made of things which are visible."*   (Hebrews 11:3)

God's Word in creation was so powerful and effective because it was backed by His inherent authority. God spoke and it was so. In the first chapter of the book of Genesis we repeatedly have the words *'And God said . . . and it was so.'* Therefore, we know that the spoken Word (not the deed) is the creating power: the Word comes before the deed: the Word produces the deed because it is supported by God's authority.

We note that God spoke in authority eight times during the creation of the world and each word produced a corresponding new state in the world. Throughout the first chapter of Genesis we see these words repeated time and again:

> *"Then God said..."*
> (Genesis 1:3; 1:6; 1:9; 1:11; 1:14; 1:20; 1:24; 1:26)

Notice that God spoke a blessing upon that which His Word had produced, i.e. the world. The blessing came when God pronounced *"it was very good"*.

> *"God saw everything that He had made, and indeed it was very good."* (Genesis 1:31)

God-given "Inherent Authority"

As well as society delegating authority to certain people within a community, we find that there are also positions of inherent authority given to certain roles within society. For example, the Prime Minister would have an authority which is inherent to his position as would, of course, the Queen.

In the same manner God Himself has given to certain people an inherent authority. This is an authority which is given and recognised by God: an authority which comes with the role. Parental authority would come into this category. Such an inherent authority has a tremendous potential for blessing, especially as far as words are concerned.

Parental Authority

Scripture gives us many such instances of fathers and mothers speaking words of blessing into their children's lives. We see this inherent parental authority and blessing through the actions of the father and mother of Rebekah (Laban and Bethuel) who spoke out their blessing on Rebekah on her forthcoming marriage to Isaac:

> *"So they sent away Rebekah their sister and her nurse, and Abraham's servant and his men. And they blessed Rebekah and* **said to her:**
>
> > *'Our sister, may you become*
> > *The mother of thousands of ten thousands;*
> > *And may your descendants possess*
> > *The gates of those who hate them.' "*
>
> (Genesis 24:59–60, emphasis added)

Likewise Laban, the father of Rachel and Leah, arose very early in the morning in order to bless his daughters before they left his home to travel away with Jacob:

> *"And early in the morning Laban arose, and kissed his sons and daughters and blessed them. Then Laban departed and returned to his place."*   (Genesis 31:55)

A Father-in-Law's Blessing

The Scriptures also encourage us to believe that a father-in-law has an inherent authority to bless his son or daughter-in-law:

> *"So Moses went and returned to Jethro his father-in-law, and said to him, 'Please let me go and return to my brethren who are in Egypt, and see whether they are still alive.' And Jethro said to Moses, 'Go in peace.' "*   (Exodus 4:18)

A Husband's Blessing

We know of course that God has given an inherent authority to husbands to speak words of blessing upon their wives:

> *"Her children rise up and call her blessed;*
> *Her husband also, and he praises her."* (Proverbs 31:28)

It is an interesting fact that the Scriptures seem to lay great store upon the power and influence of a husband's prayers for his wife. We see an example of this in Isaac's desperate prayers for Rebekah who couldn't conceive:

> *"Now Isaac pleaded with the LORD for his wife, because she was barren; and the LORD granted his plea, and Rebekah his wife conceived."* (Genesis 25:21)

A Grandfather's Blessing

Grandparents, and especially grandfathers, also have an inherent authority before the Lord in order that they might bless their grandchildren. Jacob was encouraged to do this by his son Joseph:

> *"And Joseph said to his father, 'They are my sons, whom God has given me in this place.' And he said, 'Please bring them to me, and I will bless them.'"* (Genesis 48:9)

When Joseph brought his sons to his father, Jacob, in order that he might indeed bless them, Jacob spoke out a wonderful grandfatherly blessing:

> "God, before whom my fathers Abraham and Isaac walked,
> The God who has fed me all my life long to this day,
> The Angel who has redeemed me from all evil,
> Bless the lads;
> Let my name be named upon them,
> And the name of my fathers Abraham and Isaac;
> And let them grow into a multitude in the midst of the earth."
>
> (Genesis 48:15–16)

I love the phrase *"Bless the lads"* because it sounds very much like the idiom of my grandfather who was from Wearside in County Durham and would have said something very similar concerning his grandchildren!

Jacob continued with his blessing, putting the youngest grandson before the eldest:

> "So he blessed them that day, saying, 'By you Israel will bless, saying, "May God make you as Ephraim and as Manasseh!" – '
> And thus he set Ephraim before Manasseh." (Genesis 48:20)

The words of a grandparent can be very powerful either for good or ill. Speaking from personal experience, I remember many of the words which my grandfather pronounced over me which have truly been a foundation of blessing throughout my life.

A Leader's Blessing

According to the Scriptures leaders are in a prime position to speak words of blessing into people's lives. For example, in the Scriptures we see that the priest is in a special position of leadership and as such his words have the power to bless.

A Priest's Blessing

The priests were God's representatives and they had inherent authority to speak a blessing of peace upon the congregation:

> *"Speak to Aaron and his sons, saying, 'This is the way you shall bless the children of Israel. Say to them:*
>
> > *"The LORD bless you and keep you;*
> > *The LORD make His face shine upon you,*
> > *And be gracious to you;*
> > *The LORD lift up His countenance upon you,*
> > *And give you peace." ' "* (Numbers 6:23–26)

And so Aaron, as a priest, blessed the people:

> *"Then Aaron lifted his hand toward the people, blessed them . . . "*
> (Leviticus 9:22)

When Hannah was distraught because she couldn't have children, Eli the priest spoke words of blessing over her:

> *"Then Eli answered and said, 'Go in peace, and the God of Israel grant your petition which you have asked of Him.' "*
> (1 Samuel 1:17)

These words had the power to lift Hannah from a place of deep sorrow and suffering into one of hope and expectancy.

John Kilpatrick, pastor of Brownsville Assembly of God Church in Pensacola, Florida, lists "priestly blessing" as one of the keys to the revival which broke out in his church on the 18th of June 1995.[1]

A King's Blessing

Under God we see that kings are also in a position of authority and thus King David blesses the people and his household:

> *"And when David had finished offering burnt offerings and peace offerings, he blessed the people in the name of the LORD of hosts."*
> (2 Samuel 6:18)

David, of course, also had the authority to bless his household as a husband:

> *"Then David returned to bless his household. And Michal the daughter of Saul came out to meet David . . . "* (2 Samuel 6:20)

King Solomon blessed the people:

> *"Then the king turned around and blessed the whole assembly of Israel, while all the assembly of Israel was standing."*
> (1 Kings 8:14)

The Blessing of Jesus

Jesus is the prime example of one who moved in great authority and blessed people through His words:

> *"Then they were all amazed and spoke among themselves, saying, 'What a word this is! For with authority and power He commands the unclean spirits, and they come out.'"* (Luke 4:36)

Jesus based His authority on the fact that He was a Son of the Father – His was both inherent as well as delegated authority:

"While he was still speaking, behold, a bright cloud overshadowed them; and suddenly a voice came out of the cloud, saying, 'This is My beloved Son, in whom I am well pleased. Hear Him!'"

(Matthew 17:5)

As a Son He had an inherent authority but He was also aware that He only had authorization to do what He saw the Father doing (delegated authority):

"Then Jesus said to them ... 'I do nothing of Myself; but as My Father taught Me, I speak these things.'" (John 8:28)

Jesus is also described as a great High Priest and as such He has the authority to bless His followers:

"And He led them out as far as Bethany, and He lifted up His hands and blessed them." (Luke 24:50)

He also is a King with great and total authority. The wonderful truth is that He has delegated authority to those who follow Him:

"And Jesus came and spoke to them, saying, 'All authority has been given to Me in heaven and on earth. Go therefore and make disciples of all the nations, baptizing them in the name of the Father and of the Son and of the Holy Spirit, teaching them to observe all things that I have commanded you; and lo, I am with you always, even to the end of the age.' Amen." (Matthew 28:18–20)

"Behold, I give you the authority to trample on serpents and scorpions, and over all the power of the enemy, and nothing shall by any means hurt you." (Luke 10:19)

The authority which we have been given through Jesus manifests itself in a number of ways. For instance we are:

Created Creators

We have been made in the image of God and thus we are **created creators**. How do we create? We create out of our spirit by speaking things into being according to God's Word. In the Scriptures there is an immense emphasis upon the spoken word. Why is this? It would seem to be that speaking out God's truth is a spiritual act of taking and using by faith that which God has promised will be, with the proviso that God has spoken the *rhema* Word to us in the first place as an individual and not just a collective word for everyone. As it says in the Scriptures:

> *". . . man shall not live by bread alone; but man lives by every word that proceeds from the mouth of the LORD."*
>
> (Deuteronomy 8:3)

Before we can speak God's Word with authority we need to hear the Word of God spoken to us by the Holy Spirit. As Steve Sampson says in his book *You Can Hear the Voice of God*,[2] "You must hear the Holy Spirit (the author of Scripture) in your particular situation."

Not only do we need to hear the Holy Spirit but we also need to speak out what He says in order for blessings to follow.

Children of God

We have also been given authority as **children of God**:

"But as many as received Him, to them He gave the right to become children of God, to those who believe in His name: who were born, not of blood, nor of the will of the flesh, nor of the will of man, but of God." (John 1:12–13)

As God's children we have been given the right to speak in His name, with the proviso that, like Jesus, we only speak what the Father gives us to speak, which means, of course, that we need to spend much time in His presence in order to listen to His heart.

As His children we have also been given authority to bless others by commanding demons to depart and diseases to be healed:

"Then He called His twelve disciples together and gave them power and authority over all demons, and to cure diseases." (Luke 9:1)

Priests and Kings

We are also described in the Scriptures as both **priests and kings** and as such we have the inherent authority that comes with these roles. We are told in the book of Revelation that Jesus:

"has made us kings and priests to His God and Father, to Him be glory and dominion forever and ever. Amen." (Revelation 1:6)

As such we are able to bless others with our words of *shalom*. According to the *Wycliffe Bible Commentary* the word *shalom* is a much more comprehensive word than "peace". It also includes the concepts of completeness, security, health, tranquillity, contentment, friendship, and peace with God and man. What a privilege we have been given as priests to speak such words of blessing to the people whom we meet.

> *"But you are a chosen generation, a royal priesthood."*
>
> (1 Peter 2:9)

Blessing God

We are also encouraged to:

> *"Bless God in the congregations."*   (Psalm 68:26)

There are many references in the Scriptures as to how our words have the potential of blessing God:

> *"And He led them out as far as Bethany, and He lifted up His hands and blessed them. Now it came to pass, while He blessed them, that He was parted from them and carried up into heaven. And they worshipped Him, and returned to Jerusalem with great joy, and were continually in the temple praising and blessing God."*
>
> (Luke 24:50–53)

Blessing our Enemies

With our words we are even commanded to bless our enemies:

> *"But I say to you, love your enemies, bless those who curse you, do good to those who hate you, and pray for those who spitefully use you and persecute you."*   (Matthew 5:44)

> *"Bless those who persecute you; bless and do not curse."*
>
> (Romans 12:14)

Blessing the Jewish Nation

We are encouraged to bless the Jewish people and we are told that that will bring a blessing upon ourselves:

> *"I will make you a great nation;*
> *I will bless you*
> *And make your name great;*
> *And you shall be a blessing.*
> *I will bless those who bless you,*
> *And I will curse him who curses you;*
> *And in you all the families of the earth shall be blessed."*
>
> (Genesis 12:2–3)

Blessing the Sick

We are also confident that our words can bless those who are sick, for our words will have the potential of bringing them into a state of health:

> *"Pleasant words are like a honeycomb,*
> *Sweetness to the soul and health to the bones."* (Proverbs 16:24)

A very good friend of ours, a Methodist Minister, developed very bad pains in his chest. His doctor did some tests and eventually diagnosed angina. Our friend was not convinced that it was angina and so he eventually went to stay at a Healing Centre at Crowhurst. The man in charge of the ministry there was chatting to him one day and asked him: "Who stabbed you in the chest?" Our friend remembered that a number of months prior to feeling the pain, a church steward had poked him in the chest about some church matter, saying angrily: "You'll suffer for this." The man in charge at Crowhurst prayed for him – he figuratively removed the arrows from his chest and prayed healing and the blessing of health into him. Our friend can now run up hills and go for long walks without getting out of breath and he has had no more pain. Thus we have a clear example of a person in leadership (a church steward) who used his words in a wrong manner to bring disease upon someone and another person in leadership who used his words to bless him. Thus our words have the potential to be a blessing or a curse.

Notes _____

1. John Kilpatrick, *Feast of Fire*, Marshall Pickering, 1995.
2. Steve Sampson, *You Can Hear the Voice of God*, Sovereign World, 2003.

Source from which Words Proceed

The second reason why our words are so powerful and effective is because of the source from which they proceed. From where do our words originate? Do our words simply come from our mouth? Do they come from our soul area – our minds, our emotions or our will? Or do they come from the very centre of our being – from our heart – from our innermost being?

I believe that words emanate from the very heart of a person and therefore the power of the word lies in the fact that they are touched by the state of the heart of the other person. If the words come from a critical hard heart they will have the potential of bringing a curse; if they come from a gentle loving heart they will have the potential of bringing a blessing. Therefore the words which are spoken by another person can touch my inner being for either good or ill.

Thus we see that our words have the potential of bringing forth much blessing and fruitfulness into the lives of other people. The River of Life in the Scriptures is very often a picture of the work of the Holy Spirit. For our words to bless others our words need to flow from the Holy Spirit and then they will be life-giving and a blessing to other people.

In the Scriptures Jesus is described as the Word of God:

"In the beginning was the Word, and the Word was with God, and the Word was God. He was in the beginning with God. All things were made through Him, and without Him nothing was made that was made."   (John 1:1–3)

And truly through His words much healing ensued: Jesus knew the power of words; He often spoke to the condition with which He was faced. Sometimes His Word was a word of rebuke. For example, He rebuked a fever:

"So He stood over her and rebuked the fever, and it left her."
(Luke 4:39)

He also rebuked a demon and the person was delivered:

"But Jesus rebuked him, saying, 'Be quiet, and come out of him!' "
(Mark 1:25)

Sometimes He spoke a Word of healing, as He did to a leper:

"Then Jesus put out His hand and touched him, saying, 'I am willing; be cleansed.' Immediately his leprosy was cleansed."
(Matthew 8:3)

And also to the centurion:

"And Jesus said to him, 'I will come and heal him.' The centurion answered and said, 'Lord, I am not worthy that You should come under my roof. But only speak a word, and my servant will be healed.' "   (Matthew 8:7–8)

He spoke a word of healing to some blind men:

> *"And when He had come into the house, the blind men came to Him. And Jesus said to them, 'Do you believe that I am able to do this?' They said to Him, 'Yes, Lord.' Then He touched their eyes, saying, 'According to your faith let it be to you.' And their eyes were opened."* (Matthew 9:28–30)

We need to learn how to direct our words into a person's inner being – to speak life, healing, freedom and blessing into them.

Conversely, of course, our words can become a curse rather than a blessing. According to Proverbs 18:21:

> *"Death and life are in the power of the tongue."*

So we see that it is possible to speak either words of life and blessing into another's life or speak death and a curse.

Until a certain age parents are as God to a child and if our parents have made pronouncements over us in the past, such as, "You're useless, hopeless, you're no good, you're pathetic, and nobody will ever want to marry you," we believe them and the words have the potential of going straight into our spirit. We begin to live according to their expectation of us.

Likewise the pronouncements of a husband or wife can also go very deep, for example, if there is verbal abuse by one spouse to the other using such words as: "You are pathetic," "You're a slob," "You're not a man, you're a mouse."

We have already noted the important place of authority that a grandparent has in a child's life. One woman who could never understand why she lived her life cloaked in deep shame was very interested to be told by her mother that she was illegitimate and that her grandfather had spoken words of shame over her whilst she was in the womb: "This child is a disgrace to this family – get out of my sight, I don't want to see it." One can understand why she lived her life cloaked in shame.

A baby can perceive in its young spirit much more than we maybe realise. So, if a baby hears such words as: "I hate this baby; he will never amount to anything," that pronouncement can have a long and lasting effect upon its young life.

However, the words of any authority figures can have a lasting and devastating effect. A lady, who I will call Elsie, was shattered when her first baby died of cot death when it was only four months old. She went to bed every evening, very distressed, telling her husband that she didn't want to wake up the next morning. One night the Lord came to her, wrapped her in a blanket of love, and she woke her husband to tell him it was all right although she still suffered great pain and grief.

Her grief had been deepened by her doctor saying to her one day, regarding her baby's death: "That's the worst of you modern mothers. You won't pick up your babies if they cry." That was not true of her, but she said that for twenty-one years she couldn't pass a crying baby without a great and an overwhelming longing to pick it up and feeling guilty for not doing so. It is interesting that by that time her baby would have been an adult!

The novelist Fay Weldon writes of when her husband was referred to a therapist after a minor heart attack. The therapist decided that Fay was the problem and that she and her husband were incompatible. The headline stated: "A therapist told her husband that their passion was a lie, and heartbreak and divorce followed."[1]

Inner Vows

It would appear, therefore, that our words have the ability to either bless or to curse other people or even ourselves. Inner vows are words, which we speak against ourselves very often as young children, and since they often come out of a wounded heart they bind themselves to us for the rest of our lives until God sets us free. For example: "I'm no good," "I'll never marry," "I'll never cry again," "I'll never trust a woman again," "No woman is ever going to tell me what to do," "I look awful," "I'll never make old bones!"

A woman who, as a little girl, saw her mother go into spontaneous labour vowed, "I'm never going to have children." And she never did!

The Power of God's Word

God's Word is a very powerful tool in the healing ministry. In fact, it is so powerful that it is able to divide between spirit and soul, thus enabling God to touch other people in their human spirits, through us, as we speak the Word of God into their lives. The Scriptures are described as the "sword of the Holy Spirit":

> "... the sword of the Spirit, which is the word of God."
>
> (Ephesians 6:17)

> "For the word of God is living and powerful, and sharper than any two-edged sword, piercing even to the division of soul and spirit, and of joints and marrow, and is a discerner of the thoughts and intents of the heart."
>
> (Hebrews 4:12)

Healing

We are told that God's Word brings healing:

> *"He sent His word and healed them."*   (Psalm 107:20)

Life-giving

God's Word is Life-giving:

> *"holding fast the word of life, so that I may rejoice in the day of Christ . . . "*   (Philippians 2:16)

Jesus said:

> *"The words that I speak to you are spirit, and they are life."*
>   (John 6:63)

Creative

God's Word is creative: it brings into being things which are not. We have already seen that God created the world through His Word – the uncreated Creator created out of His Spirit through His Word:

> *"By faith we understand that the worlds were framed by the word of God, so that the things which are seen were not made of things which are visible."*   (Hebrews 11:3)

Therefore, we know that the spoken word (not the deed) is the creating power; the word comes before the deed; the word produces the deed.

The Place of Faith

Faith is the bridge between knowing your authority, knowing the will of the Father, and speaking it into being. Faith reaches out to God – receives the word from Him and speaks it into being. You cannot speak into existence what you have not received by faith, nor can you keep it within you because then it will not achieve what God intended.

*Notes*_____

1. *The Times* newspaper, times 2, 6th September, 2005, p. 4.

Keys to Freedom

The Tree of Life

There is a very interesting reference in the Scriptures to the fact that our tongue is like a tree of life, and knowing how to use our tongues in a positive way is the route to freedom, both for ourselves and for other people for whom we may be called upon to pray.

> *"A wholesome tongue is a tree of life."* (Proverbs 15:4)

According to the well known and respected commentator C.J. Ellicott, a wholesome tongue is "one which heals and soothes by its gentleness and judicious words".[1] It is interesting to trace the references to the tree of life throughout the Scriptures as to what its properties are and what effect it has upon a situation or person. The tree of life is, of course, mentioned in the first and the last books of the Bible. In Genesis chapter 2 we have the first reference to this tree, where we are told that:

> *"The tree of life was also in the midst of the garden."* (Genesis 2:9)

Whilst in the last book of the Bible we learn that:

> *"In the middle of its street, and on either side of the river, was the tree of life, which bore twelve fruits, each tree yielding its fruit every month. The leaves of the tree were for the healing of the nations."*
>
> (Revelation 22:2)

Matthew Henry, commentating upon this passage, writes:

> "As to this tree, observe,
>
> 1. The situation of it . . . This tree of life is fed by the pure waters of the river that comes from the throne of God.
> 2. The fruitfulness of this tree. (1) It brings forth many sorts of fruit – twelve sorts, suited to the refined taste of all the saints. (2) It brings forth fruit at all times – yields its fruit every month. This tree is never empty, never barren; there is always fruit upon it." [2]

What a wonderful thought that because our tongue is a tree of life it can speak life into the inward parts. This is especially true of speaking and affirming God's Word to our spirits.

> *"And you shall know the truth, and the truth shall make you free."*
>
> (John 8:32)

By taking hold of one of God's promises and affirming it to our inner man we will find the freedom that God's Word brings.

However, it is also true of our own words, for example by speaking such encouraging words as, "I can do it", "I like the way I did that", "I can do all things through Christ who strengthens me," we can move from a position of weakness to a position of strength. Positive words are powerful and life-enhancing.

On the other hand, we can also use our tongues against ourselves! Negative words can speak lies into our spirits: one man who said about himself, "I may as well be dead," had a stroke three days later and was dead within the month. Another person frequently said about himself, "I'm out of here," and in fact moved away from his good position of employment shortly afterwards. Our words are meant to encourage, affirm, build up, challenge and speak truth both into our lives and also into the lives of other people. Some of us will need to repent for the words we have used to poison, wound or damage ourselves or other people!

The Word of God

One of the most important keys to being freed from the effects of damaging and negative words is to allow Jesus Himself, who is the Word of God, to speak truth into the inner being of a person through the Holy Spirit. He can reach down into our innermost depths and supplant the darkness with the light of His truth, thus bringing His Kingdom into every part of us:

> *"The entrance of Your words gives light;*
> *It gives understanding to the simple."* (Psalm 119:130)

How does Jesus do that? He does it by opening our under-standing to His truth through the Scriptures. It is important to remember that, even in the natural world, for our minds to understand something it takes another mind to explain it to us. Thus we rely on the mind of the Holy Spirit to inform our minds of the truth of the Scriptures which He has inspired as well as the truth of any painful situation which we may find ourselves in.

The Holy Spirit also brings revelation into our human spirits through His Word. The Holy Spirit takes the inspired Word from the Scriptures and plants it firmly into our human spirits thus displacing the lies, which we have believed, with His truth.

Jesus the Light of the World

Sometimes the Lord, as the Light of the World, will include another person in order to bring truth and light to the one in need. This would especially be true where the wounding from negative words has gone very deep. For example, the way in which I would proceed if I was ministering to someone would be as follows:

- After the person has shared the situation with me we would spend a little time waiting upon the Holy Spirit for His guidance.
- As we wait He may bring a memory to the surface that has a number of buried lies, negative words, curses and darkness within.
- I would ask Him to enter the "memory room" as the Light of the World and reveal the truth and the lies and negativity which are in that room.
- With the person's involvement and permission I will ask the Holy Spirit to challenge the lies and confront the darkness and begin to bring His truth to the fore.

When I was ministering in one church in Canada a lady came forward for ministry. She was absolutely heartbroken because her cat had died. As she shared her story with me I felt quite distinctly that she was suffering from a deeper grief than that for her beloved cat. She told me a little of her life story and then we decided to wait upon the Holy Spirit for more insight. As we waited she suddenly began to sob even more. After a while she shared the memory which the Holy Spirit was bringing to the surface. It was of a time when she was fifteen and quite permissive and rebellious. She had had a number of sexual partners and eventually went on to have an abortion. She had subsequently become a Christian. During the following year she convinced herself that she had never had an abortion, that she was unlovable and that the only one that could possibly love her was her cat. That is why the death of her cat was so devastating. As the Holy Spirit revealed the truth to her she acknowledged the truth about her baby and began to move into true grief. The Holy Spirit then revealed how much God loved and forgave her and wanted to restore her.

- I would break the power of any negative words or curses which the person has believed.
- The person will then need to work with the Holy Spirit in refuting the lies of the enemy as well as the human lies which he or she has swallowed and replace them with the truth of the Word of God.

"You shall know the truth, and the truth shall make you free."
(John 8:32)

– **Negative words**: "I'll never forgive myself."

God's Word says:

> "'*Come now, and let us reason together,*'
> *Says the* LORD,
> '*Though your sins are like scarlet,*
> *They shall be as white as snow;*
> *Though they are red like crimson,*
> *They shall be as wool.*'" (Isaiah 1:18)

– **Negative words**: "I can't do anything."

God's Word says:

> "*I can do all things through Christ who strengthens me.*"
> (Philippians 4:13)

– **Negative words**: "I'll never be free."

God's Word says:

> "*If the Son makes you free, you shall be free indeed.*"
> (John 8:36)

– **Negative words**: "I am really frightened."

God's Word says:

> "*Fear not, for I have redeemed you;*
> *I have called you by your name;*
> *You are Mine.*" (Isaiah 43:1)

– **Negative words**: "God cannot love me."

God's Word says:

> "*I have loved you with an everlasting love.*"
> (Jeremiah 31:3)

- **Negative words**: "I am all alone."

  God's Word says:

  > *"He Himself has said, 'I will never leave you nor forsake you.'"* (Hebrews 13:5)

- **Negative words**: "I am not worth anything."

  God's Word says:

  > *"Since you were precious in My sight,*
  > *You have been honoured,*
  > *And I have loved you."* (Isaiah 43:4)

- **Negative words**: "It's impossible."

  God's Word says:

  > *"The things which are impossible with men are possible with God."* (Luke 18:27)

- Thus Jesus, who is the Truth, the Holy Spirit who is the Spirit of Truth, and the Word of God, which is the Word of Truth, will move the person into the place of wholeness.

Finally, we would do well to take note of God's way of blessing and speak it to ourselves and to others as the opportunity arises:

> *"And the LORD spoke to Moses, saying: 'Speak to Aaron and his sons, saying, "This is the way you shall bless the children of Israel. Say to them:*
>
> *'The LORD bless you and keep you;*
> *The LORD make His face shine upon you,*
> *And be gracious to you;*
> *The LORD lift up His countenance upon you,*
> *And give you peace.'"'"* (Numbers 6:22–26)

Questions to Consider

- What lies or half-truths have you swallowed? Ask the Holy Spirit for revelation.
- How do you use the sword of your spirit – your tongue?
  - Do you seek to encourage yourself?
  - Do you slander yourself?
  - Do you use threats against yourself?
  - Do you build yourself up or tear yourself down?
  - Do you build others up or pull them down?
- What hurtful words have you said recently?
  Seek forgiveness.
- What hurtful words have been said over you?
  Offer forgiveness.
- What positive words have you spoken so far today?
  Be encouraged.

Ask the Holy Spirit for a verse from Scripture to take with you into the coming week.

Notes _____

1. C.J. Ellicott, DD, (editor), *Bible Commentary, Volume 4*, Cassell and Co. Ltd.
2. Matthew Henry's *Commentary, Volume 10*, William Mackenzie, London.

Appendix:

Family Lines of Adam, Abraham and Rahab

Adam's Family Line

- Adam was 130 years old when Seth was born
- Adam was 235 when Enosh was born
- Adam was 325 when Kenan was born
- Adam was 395 when Mahalalel was born
- Adam was 460 when Jared was born
- **Adam was 622 when Enoch was born**
- Adam was 687 when Methuselah was born
- Adam was 874 when Lamech was born
- Adam didn't see Noah born –
- Adam died 126 years before Noah's birth aged 930

Figure 3: Adam's Family Line

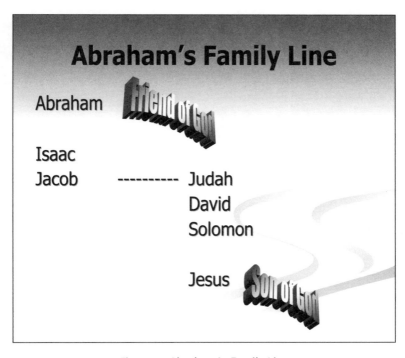

Figure 4: Abraham's Family Line

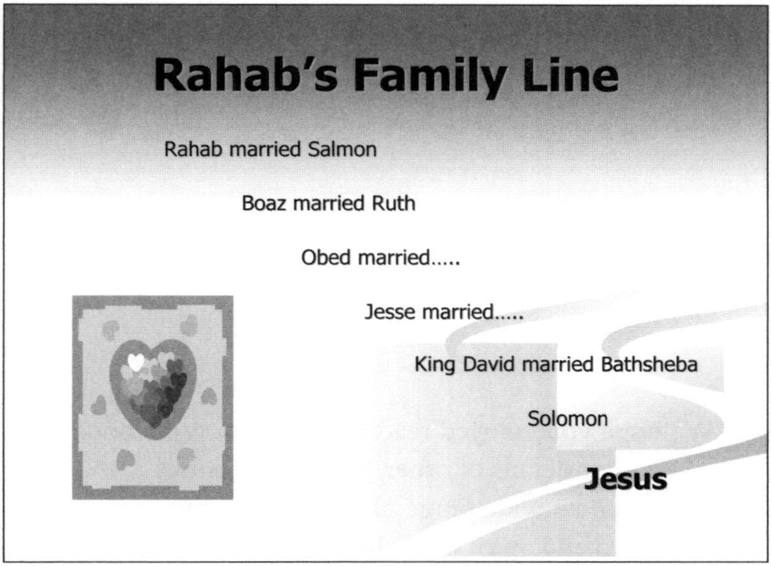

Rahab's Family Line

Rahab married Salmon

Boaz married Ruth

Obed married.....

Jesse married.....

King David married Bathsheba

Solomon

Jesus

Figure 5: Rahab's Family Line

We hope you enjoyed reading this New Wine book.
For details of other New Wine books
and a wide range of titles from other
Word and Spirit publishers visit our website:
www.newwineministries.co.uk
email: newwine@xalt.co.uk